The

accident

of

birth

Other poetry collections by the same author:

pebbles, debris (2003)

Dealing with the edge (2011)

Les chemins d'ici/The roads round here (2016)

The accident of birth

Poems

Jim Dening

Arcade Publishers
2020

The accident of birth: first published 2020 by Arcade Publishers, The Tannery, The Frith, Ledbury HR8 1LW, UK.

Text typeset in Garamond 12pt, titles in 18pt italic.

Printed on acid-free long life paper and bound in England by Orphans Press, Leominster HR6 0LD, UK.

A catalogue record for this book is available from the British Library. ISBN 978-0-9560714-5-3

Contents

Contents

Contents

I

Observations

All torn up

One of those brilliant autumn days,
I was full of emotion about it,
anxious to shift the sublime onto paper.
Even the early morning was dazzling,
you could only glance with guarded eyes
where a vivid haze obscured the forest crest.
Mist sidled down between the vines
like pale fur; at the village
wood smoke rising caught new air
above the hill and veered away.
This time of year, round here,
it is silvery toward the sun all day;
the sky is blanched, the branches blurred,
only with your back against the light
can you see some colour in the world.

A track comes down the hill,
more a firebreak than a track
and cut by torrents after rain;
we walk there sometimes, and the top
will take you over to the road
and the ravine; where the gorge is wide
and the rock face highest on the other side,
there the speculative eagles hang,
a whole valley for a single pair.
Nearby the ancient route began,
to Sisteron and the Route des Alpes,
beyond the carry of the drifting smoke.

The brilliance was coming to its setting point;
to the edge it came, the dazzling swathe
like the bursting light in the Battle of Algiers*
pouring towards us, constrained
in a violent ironic cruciform;
here the hilltop is the only limit,
and if you look, you stay blinking
at a green and purple imprint of the sun.
Now a shadow overtook my glass of wine,
a chill fell on the table top,
I was disheartened and outraged
by impotence, tore up the useless words,
but vanity then wrote them out again.

* French film, dir. Pontecorvo, 1966

At Symonds Yat

Through the hanging hillside woods,
past the lime kilns in the rock,
down a narrow path to the river bank,
the ancient way.

Sitting on the narrow landing stage,
dangling our feet above the water
where minnows dart among the weeds,
we are waiting.

We had waved and whistled, but
no one appears on the other side,
so we sit and gaze across the river
moving past us.

Shadows begin to fall upon us
in the steep valley where the river runs;
twelve thousand years ago wild cats and men
lived in caves nearby.

Above our heads the rope across the river
is tethered to its post; other ropes
have stretched above the water
since Roman times.

There is movement on the other side,
the ferryman unchains his boat! and slowly
hauls his loop around the crossing rope
towards us.

I pay our fare, not in obols
but in new sovereigns of this world;
and as we cross the slow water is dark
around the boat.

There is merriment among the spirits
on the other side; amid the company
the ferryman is gone and our return
appears uncertain.

We cannot stay among these shadows;
at the water's edge we wait again
and look across to where we were
when we were younger.

Climbing down

– How fearful
And dizzy 'tis to cast one's eyes so low!
The crows and choughs that wing the midway air
Show scarce so gross as beetles...
King Lear, Act IV, Scene 6.

Going up was easy, quick
from ledge to ledge and grip to grip,
gaining rapid height.

A seagull floats beside,
while far far down another wave
is breaking over rocks.

Breath stops. Movement stops.
Fear like water loosens strength.
The surface flakes, crumbs of stone

come falling from above,
a few feet below the edge
and all above is overhang.

The idea of letting go.
Fingers and toes are locked,
dare not look up or down,

a voice – it is your own, you fool –
is whispering: be still, be present,
imagine moving so slowly

you scarcely seem to move;
be as imperceptible as
the fingers on a clock.

Freed from time, inch by inch
he feels his way and downward creeps;
slowly past the midway air, so slow

a beetle walks upon his hand;
slowly past a hundred million years
in layers of chalky animals;

so close against the rock, at times
his face, his mouth are pressed upon it;
closely past each grassy tuft, so close

he tastes the very sea upon it;
sometimes he dare not move at all,
and hangs there, waiting.

Fragile vessels

After seeing finds from a sunken Roman vessel in a museum in Villa Joyosa, Spain

The fish have swum among them
for two thousand years as they lie scattered
after bursting from the sinking ship.

The ship remains spreadeagled
beneath lead ingots in the hold
and amphorae among its timbers.

In dim green photographs
the rounded pointed forms of the amphorae
spill across the seabed.

This was a cargo of fish paste,
the delectable repellent *garum* beloved by Romans
to render old meat palatable.

Fragments of broken amphorae
were used for making walls and roads,
they are mere clay vessels, after all.

It came about in the museum
that I walked among the amphorae, and saw
the trails of sea-worms upon them,

the dried moulds and scrapings,
and touched their rough clay, felt the curves,
and peered inside to listen for an echo.

I heard the voices of Iberian slaves,
filling them and caulking them; and the cursing
as heavy weights were carted off.

Later, after the violence of the storm,
there came the silence of slipping through the waters
toward their resting place.

We touch things in order to make them,
such as bread or clay; but touching these old pots
does not make them live again.

They signal the departure of their people,
they signal that we are fragile vessels and will be broken,
and fish will swim among the fragments.

Herefordshire ways of looking at a barn

For twenty years we've come past here
(the walkers say), while leaning on their sticks,
and two old dogs are anxious to agree;
it's been a landmark for us of a sort
beneath its rust-red corrugated roof,
subsiding broken-jointed into earth.

Two hundred years, who knows, and more,
this place has stood rough-built beside the track
(the orchard grower says), the old carts
went up for charcoal and coppiced staves,
deepening the holloway between the trees,
while overhead the buzzard hangs and mews.

First thing here was get the levels right
(the builder says), we had the digger in,
a kango on the rock beneath the floor;
we must have had two hundred ton away
until we squared him up, jacked the frame,
cut out the rot and spliced the new oak in.

Wormholes (the sand blaster says) go barely
half an inch, old oak inside still breaks the drill.
We made new ironwork (the blacksmith says),
catches and handles all beaten and swaged.
Tiling's finished (the roofer says), I'll fix
the downpipe at the gulley and flaunch him in.

Where has the old barn gone? (say the owl and the swallow,
the bat, the badger, the weasel, the fox and the rabbit),
where are our burrows and perches, where are the ivy
and old smells and dark corners? Where is our home?

Magpies

A chattering mass of magpies
has just descended from the church
and jostles in the road outside.
More keep coming to join the crowd
clapping shoulders and hailing friends.
Men are loosening black ties
stocky big hands they roll and sway
squinting and coughing down their smokes.
The women stand together
legs planted arms folded tattoos
disappearing under white blouses.
Will the old man be scattered
or travel onward in a bucket
swinging from the axle?

The city

In recollection of Émile Verhaeren, *La ville tentaculaire* (1895)

Travellers would have seen the city
rising in the distance
amid towers and turrets and smoke;
now upon the old flood plain
squat the developers' estates
weighed down by concrete and pretension.

Along the highways, over bridges,
vehicles stream and weave,
they bunch and pause and move again;
a lorry may have overturned,
goods lie scattered or a body lies,
sirens and flashing lights approach.

Arriving at a station in the centre
we stagger from the train
into the cacophony of noise;
the violence of announcements in the ears,
the trundling cases and the voices,
hundreds of voices raised over voices.

Outside the station the people are surging
in the road, eyes on phones, teeth bared
in sidelong shouts of conversation;
ravenously they descend
on shops and bars, unsatisfied
they obstruct the seething street.

Behind the shops and fashion-decked façades,
in the alleys and the smelly yards,
up the steps and below decaying doors
brown furry backs slither and squeak
into the warehouse, the garage,
the toilet and underneath the bed.

The ghosts of the city are burnt ash,
they walk the streets among us,
they sometimes leave a stain upon the road;
older souls lie in the city cemeteries,
having proved their vices and corruption,
they lie mouldering and do not speak.

The hopsack race

By God they were merry
when we came into the bar,
a circle of enormous blokes
lining up pints of Wye Valley
and Ludlow Gold, wearing huge
blue teeshirts with Pipsqueak's Pullers
or some such message on the back,
and drinking as fast as they could laugh.

No wonder they were thirsty,
they had run or limped or staggered
the Bromyard hopsack race;
you can imagine the picture of
teams of gasping shouting cursing
men in fours, coming up the High Street
past the Hop Pole past the Bay Horse
past the Falcon and the King's Arms
round the corner by the church
down the back road and round again!

A hopsack full of hops will weigh
the same as a man but he don't have
arms and legs and he don't have
handles what he has are ears
ears at each corner you have to hold
them somehow and keep running
and not let him touch the ground
or you lose time and points and honour.

In the mind's eye another image
by God of four men running
up the street shouting gasping
carrying a heavy weight between them
holding it by its arms and legs,
the brother or the cousin just caught
in some trivial back street action,
the wailing coming off the ruined walls,
keeping clear of rubble on the ground
they run for their lives and family honour.

Another round was on the counter,
the fellows were reflective for a moment;
they said: sorry, are we too loud?
– oh no, I said, you brought it all to life.

They are part of me

Following consideration of Frida Kahlo's painting: *What the water gave me VI*

Imagine a self-portrait with no face.
You have all seen my face, I stare at you
beneath my bow-shaped brow;
but you have not seen my feet
at least not my toes and my damaged toe,
but they are part of me;
or the suggestion of my legs and my damaged leg,
but they are part of me;
or the things that I love and fear,
parents, lovers, naked people,
strange places and creatures,
but they are part of me;
my body under water
has given birth to my mind.

Imagine lying in the bath
with your toes sticking out and perfectly reflected
as long as you don’t make waves;
with the far edge of the bathtub
making a frame, a round arch as if
particular concentration were needed;
but if you move, the surface will scatter
the fanciful array of images and symbols
heaped upon your legs:
an incantation of objects, as if you wish
to be cured of your life by magic.

Here are the extensions of my mind
in images upon a painted surface:
the absurd accidents of life,
the undeserved detritus:
the people, the volcano, the skyscraper,
the flowering cactus, as if to say
the spiky can give birth to radiance:
all of this scattered like toys from a hat
upon my poor legs stretched out in the bath.
I am burnt, I am salved
by the presence of the past.

To a woman wearing a top with hummingbirds on it

Motionless in motion,
you are become the image
you are wearing or rather
the symbol has settled
like a creature on your essence.

They hover vibrating
all but stationary
wings too quick to see
beaks tasting the nectar
of a strange flower.

Your choice reinforces
the idea that is you, suspended
you live in the moment
of the bird, and sip
at the flower's heart.

Where they hang and echo

Between a barn and a cowshed
he hears – he hears again –
the buzzard's cry, and sees high up
against the cloud the bird's wide wings
where it hangs and mews.

He stands with legs apart
and arms spread wide
in an image of St Francis
and he calls – he whistles:
peeeuuuuuw! peeeuuuuuw!

The buzzard turns – it turns –
and motionless in its glide
this bird of prey descends
and hovers there
as if to see who calls –

even while he wills
the bird to come to him,
with a flicker of a wing
it is away above the woods,
its call now high and faint.

He hears new words escape
and rise towards the clouds
where they hang and echo
while below the people listen
and run to catch one
if it falls.

II

Questions

A cold sun

A cold sun glances through the trees;
along the frosted track a fluffed-up robin
and his mate the blackbird scamper
towards their meagre feast of crumbs.
The seeds have frozen in the cracked earth.
What promises, what mendacity have kept
the people quiet along their slippery streets?
What time of renewal is at hand?
Oh, we will see the season through,
with brave spirits and absurd jokes,
with our cocked heads and bright eyes,
with our mates we will see it through
as if we were all young together
and might yet lead flaming lives.

At the cathedral

In the gathering dusk
through the cathedral gardens
along the curving paths
good citizens approach and hurry
in winter coats and hats.

On benches or on the grass
beside the curving paths
young men sit or sprawl
drinking beer from cans
eyeing the citizens.

On the lawns and round the graves
not far from the great door
knots of kids laugh and jostle
the girls all legs and skittering
the boys pushing and chasing.

The new moon hangs in a cradle
above the long cathedral. The old ones
walk past the shouts of the young ones:
'fuck off!' and 'fuckin' gerroff me!'
they call joyfully to each other.

The orchestra plays strange instruments
in the dies irae. The massed choir howls
'libera me!' into the roof space.
The old folk emerge, redeemed,
avoiding beer cans on the paths.

Bearing witness

Born during a world war
becoming aware
of concentration camps
of the holocaust
of intolerance and persecution
of empire and privilege
of prejudice and exclusion
and always inequality and injustice
an only child
innocent of involvement
guilty of non-involvement
and always more disgrace
requiring witness.

How to be useful

Doing nothing
in the face of so much requiring action
at least try some protest
to show there is another way
meanwhile the many the many
inarticulate but quietly enraged
are hoping for a quiet revolution
a turnaround in values and priorities
to bring greater equality and justice
well huh! we say –
a quiet revolution?
we are waiting for it too
and what use is poetry?
as if some words unread by most
will change the laws and resolutions...
or merely spare us
from feeling useless.

In the undergrowth

For how many years have we climbed
this rough track? In the bushes at the side,
the staring and growling of a thousand
eyes and mouths. We knew the dangers,
we heard and saw the stoats and weasels
assembling in angry groups and blocking
our progress to the light. The light?
Is it any lighter now, one year
or ten years later? Are the creatures
of the undergrowth to be appeased
by argument? Or shall we turn towards them
with food and gifts and friendship? And
would this precarious unity then mean
we too must crouch in the undergrowth?

Is this a new time?

Slow winter has dawdled into spring,
a new sun arouses colour from the soil,
and carpets of forget-me-nots are laid;
in the woods the bluebells have their day,
and dandelions re-state the case for yellow.

They say the birds are singing louder than before,
and in the sunlight insects hang in clouds;
while that pair of rabbits sit beneath the blossom,
two robins perch together, a goldcrest has been seen,
and a tiny frog has ventured from his pond.

It is a new season but is it different?
Is it possible when we are quiet
and the rushing and the rumbling die away,
that we hear and see more sharply
a new kind of nature?

Let them go

Let them go for heaven's sake
you've fed them long enough
with wine and nuts and raisins
let them go to peck and squawk

let them dive like angry seagulls
upon complacency and prejudice
and waken the sleeping minds
of our brave brothers and sisters

throw them far into the crowd
throw them into their mouths
don't distract with daily images
of naked women and scurrilous events

see if the people will come running
shouting and waving their arms
see if they mount the barricades
see if anything at all will change

gather your brave words together
write new ones to inspire
hope the people we desire to love
don't kill the messenger instead.

Others think they are right

In the farrago of nonsense
there is competition for extremity
and unwitting mediocrity;
out of ignorance comes forth
conviction and from conviction
march violence and abuse
armed with absurdity and lies
and open mouths and pick handles.

Worshippers die as a church is blown up
because others think they are right;
a reporter is shot dead by youths
because others think they are right;
children are bombed in the desert
because others think they are right;
the innocent hope for acceptance
but others still think they are right.

Over there...

... or the time we went to see our friends
Brian and Flo and ate in that open-air place
high up beside the river Scheldt, and drank
beyond discretion, but not beyond friendship.
Or all the times we went to the market in Pernes,
down south, and ate at the Café de Paris in St-Didier,
where Sabine the waitress would shimmy up to us,
then roar hoarsely back to the bar: deux Ricards, deux!
Or the time we went to the funeral in Antwerp,
because you died, dammit, my best friend
and champion piss-taker, you died because
of smoking too much, or was it laughing too much.
Now we visit Flo in her new house
and embrace her with love and melancholy...

... and the times we drove onward, northbound,
to the old city of Dordrecht, to stay with
our friends Hans and Ineke in their strange house,
once the brewery of fifteenth-century monks.
And the times we walked to the square in town,
where Hans would buy small fresh herrings, which
we ate in their kitchen, with glasses of jonge jenever,
dropping the tails on the floor for scavenging cats.
And sometimes you and I would walk through town
and over bridges past the old harbour, where we sat
on a bench facing the great river Maas, waving
now and then to men on passing barges.
Once or twice, we stayed in the huge old water tower,
along the river, modestly named the Villa Augustus...

... and then the many times, crossing France,
around halfway we came to our friend's cottage,
in the middle of forests, near La Chapelle d'Angillon,
home of Alain-Fournier and le grand Meaulnes,
whose mysterious domain seemed to be nearby;
and not far away the octagonal centre of Henrichemont,
built by a minister of Louis XIV, where once we stayed
in the dark and wretched Hôtel Le Boeuf.
But with our friends, artists François and his pals
Bamba and Nicole, we were merry, we ate and drank
mushrooms and wines from the villages, while
the curious donkey in the field came to see us.
And once, as a present, I took a pot of garlic honey,
yes, garlic honey, and they devoured it avidly on the spot.

Poems mustn't preach

This is not a sermon, but
it could be a small back door
towards another life...
Go into the garden,
watch and listen,
no matter what season,
perhaps take your notebook
and copy down the chirrups
and other mysteries.
If you have no garden,
and see only glass or concrete
or a narrow staircase
or the desperation of the street,
go into yourself,
go into your inner garden,
watch and listen,
note down the chirrups
and other mysteries
of peace and beauty
in yourself.

Song of everybody else

In riposte to Walt Whitman and in ackowledgment to Richard Holloway

I celebrate all of you
I sing all who are not me
the numberless flowers of humanity
the weeds the stony ground
not just in smiling sanctity
not only in the easy fantasy
of pleasant women or like minds
but the alien the incomprehensible
the vicious the intolerant
the ignorant the fantastical
the demented the unresponsive
all of these and their ideas
all of these in their peculiarity
since the atoms or the indifferent dust
of earth and stars might as well
have composed us otherwise and will yet
and I could have been any one of you
– it is hard to acknowledge
the cruel the infamous the threatening
but can it be wrong
if forgiveness is the only way
to unlock the unforgivable?
– or must we always
in vengeance or in righteousness
take refuge in our complacent tribe?

The accident of birth

Imagine who you might have been
with different parents, different family,
another house or town or country,
another language and above all
another set of beliefs.

You wouldn't just be different;
you would be another person
with his or her particular
experience of existence,
alongside millions of others.

And of these millions,
some are kind or generous,
others are vicious and intolerant,
some are interested in difference,
others believe they are right.

But you wouldn't exist
in your bubble made by others;
so make the most of now,
appreciate your accidental gifts,
invent some ideas of your own.

The faces

The faces are coming forward in the night
from the darkness of the mind again
in the black corner behind the door;
palely illuminated, sometimes in a cluster
one above, one behind another, as if
pressing forward, eyes open, looking.

Here are those faces behind barbed wire
here is the hollow gaze of wrinkled men
expelled from tribal lands;
here are women standing in a line,
white-faced, bought and sold, abused;
sometimes strange crowds appear
of men and women and children,
gaunt and flushed, staring for their lives
across some barrier of desolation;
or the mugshots of victims
before they are taken out and shot.

Rising to the surface, the faces all unknown,
but familiar, and intimate, and always coming back.

The others

sometimes we remember the others
the unknown multitudes
who never learnt how to learn
who believe what they are told
who allow disease into their homes
landslides and hurricanes upon their houses
violence and oppression upon their families
who suffer poverty and ignorance
who cannot escape and have no choice
and imagine they are punished by god

until men hoist other men upon their shoulders
to save them from the flood or try to see ahead
dreaming instead of anxiety security
instead of the fear of god the love of man
until the rich die dreaming of chance instead of privilege
all the money in the world is not enough
until the wise die dreaming of purpose instead of prestige
all the attention in the world is not enough
and nothing makes sense of a natural process
which goes against justice and mercy

Waiting

Waiting
as if in this life
things might get better
or there be a kind of perfection
and we would be content.

We wait
and see this human nature
perform amazing acts
of courage or generosity
sustaining our patience.

We have waited
and see only
the persistence in other places
of prejudice and injustice
and ignorance.

We will wait
and as long as we deplore
in complacent self-interest
and detachment
nothing will change.

What is the question?

Something knows it is here
in a swarming assembly
of organisms animating a machine
of arms legs eyes mouth etc
much can be observed
if not understood
who this is or why
while you over there are stuck
in your own strange tower
and talking in a language
to this in here while we reflect
that a seed was planted
and around the seed
a creature grew different
in every cell from every cell
that ever existed
in all the universe
just like in the garden
creating an innumerable number
of centres of identity
some of them wondering
what they are and why
this flicker of vision
here and not there
for a moment
knowing something is going on
not knowing what the question is

When words become rabbits

When words become rabbits
they come out of their holes
and prick up their ears
and nibble the grass
and scamper about
and ecstatically mate
and go round in gangs
and carry a stick
and bite at your clothes
and spend all your money
and drink all your wine
and sleep in your bed
and rarely if ever
go back in their holes.

Rabbits… the sequel

The weather has changed overnight
the horizons are dark and obscure
the rabbits are out with their cudgels
they are taking control to be sure.
The rabbits are patrolling their borders
they are protecting their sovereign warren
they are cudgelling unwelcome vermin
and imprisoning anything foreign.
But the stoats and the weasels are watching
in their black uniforms from the wood
they sent compliments down to the rabbits
to delude them, as predators should.
Now the rabbits have sacked all their leaders
the fur is beginning to fly
some rabbits are more and more worried
they'll end up in a grand rabbit pie.

III

Reflections

Benedict's poem

For 28 November 2015

It can seem a long way
the track twisting through the trees
the sky veiled by shadows
often an inner solitude
but if you can be patient
and be by fortune blessed
around a sudden corner
there comes unexpectedly
a great space
a calm light and level road
a view to the horizon
and new flowers along the edge.

Benedict, you knew
who you were meant to be
with a cough and a nod
you chose your name
hearing it well said
and offered by your mother
to you new-born.
This is the unexpected
this is the very moment
the grasping of something new
in a handful of light
and finding that the way continues.

Conjuring the fox

Let's make the fox appear
up there before the garden shed,
imagine a chicken unsuspecting
offers itself as bait.

Here comes the tip of a nose –
no, it is a blowing leaf;
here comes a cautious paw –
no, it is a wilted flower.

You think he will not come,
the wily fox;
you can be wily too,
you can conjure him.

Close your eyes, close them
tight and wait;
surely that was a blur of fur –
wait for the air to clear...

He comes up to the window,
his eyes look into yours;
the fox nods his head,
his ears lift – he smiles.

The weather is changing,
the fox is bathed in shifting light –
he fades, he fades, he is gone;
but he came: the fox came unto you.

Delectable wasp

With acknowledgment to Bill Manhire for at least one suggestive borrowing

Through the wall people
are making couple noises
it is us heard by others
how we laughed
how we diverted ourselves
waiting for a peaceful place
amid the racket of ignorance.
Fragments of being
recurrent words
stick in the ear
like an insect
or a sting on the tongue
from a delectable wasp
in the corner of
the great wise hall;
the constant contours
of women's bodies
between the lines
like pheasants sleeping
in trees at night,
they can be caught if
made drunk with raisins
soaked in promises;
and offering oh!
pale experimental breasts
transformative
elliptical shapes
flung beyond the earth
reducing slightly
the arc of space
left inside the mind.

Don't half

Das Ewigweibliche zieht uns hinan.
[The eternal feminine draws us upward]
– the last line of Goethe's *Faust.*

The other day he said
if I die before you
you may say he used to say
I don't half love you!

– this being an old family way
of speaking from up north
entailing an assertion
negatived but redoubled
defused but emphasised
such apparent (but false)
humorous self-deprecation
also being characteristic.

After all I don't half love
a good cup of coffee
the scabious I just planted
my pickup truck
our two black cats
parts of Fidelio
the assembly of words
the French language
as well as you
all of these being
ideas which lead us
to a different order
and I can rank them
in fact I just did.

Ending

For Ian Venables

Haunting the streets of the past
I came to very few places
where I found the old warmth
of bygone friends and their graces
and have come to mourn or implore
the ghosts of their faces.

The images fade like dead leaves
in autumn, the strong winds abating
and leaving them lying in dust;
only the most precious creating
a vision of some one who
perhaps is still waiting.

In our memories are scraps of our lives
when we could be carefree and careless,
but some we cling to and guard
as if to redress an old promise,
though time and distance and loss
have wiped out all solace.

Ah, here is the very place:
we parted as if we were sleeping;
we were parted, and still now
I see beyond calling, beyond keeping
the face or its ghost look back
not smiling but weeping.

In a lighthouse

Waking up again in here,
looking out, normal feelings
and ideas within reach.

The tower sways in the wind,
waves break and pull at the foot
in strange effects of movement.

Intermediate gantries swing
shifting useful material
in big grabbers and buckets.

Where the coastline runs away
cars and people can be seen
upon it or imagined.

In the cabin the controls
will if consciously applied
adjust the structure slightly.

The lantern needs attention
if it is to continue
throwing out a beam of light.

Another lighthouse flashes
from a nearby headland.

In the south

To the desperate memory
of calmly leaving my daughter
beside the house of Signora B.
in the vague outskirts of Florence
knowing not to call her back
but drive on darkening roads
towards the Belvedere and away.

To the wistful memory
of our afternoon in Siena,
she in pleasure and innocence
I taken with the private vision
of another presence beside me once
gazing on Simone Martini's mural
of ancient siege in golds and blues

Good riddance to the memory
of Arezzo, where in ignorance
I never saw the city's ancient heart
but fell exhausted in a sad hotel,
an alsatian watching as I ate,
the blues and golds of football teams
in flickering war upon the wall.

Maybe to the ancient memory
of the reedy shores of Trasimeno
where ten thousand Roman ghosts
still stain the mud and stir the air
at evening; but drawn by the old obsession
towards Cortona and Perugia
with no one on the crowded steps.

At last the peaceful memory
of golden Urbino, where I arrived
not lured by a ghost
but to address new spirits on my own,
was rewarded by a raphaelite
vision of the heavenly body
freed of earthbound constraint.

I shall

When you my grandson
are grown beyond four years
into manhood,
into strength and beauty,
I shall be dead.
When the young tree
we planted in memory
of our friend is grown
enough to shelter you,
I shall be dead.
When I might understand
at last the patterns of life
emerging around us
on the earth,
I shall

It is all this

[after the walk from Relleu to Sella, Spain]

It is the walking
it is the skyline
the steepness of slopes
the staring at the ground
the study of stones
the stepping to a foothold
the displacement of pebbles
it is the consideration of time
the ageing of rocks
the rising of the mountain
the shaping of the terraces
it has been all this

Mending a favourite bowl

clean break simple
wash the pieces
here are the bits
here is the glue
see the colours
greens and russets
brushed and fingered
beneath the glaze
creep glue along
the longest edge
tiny amount
no squeezing out
the two bits bite
another piece
along that side
here comes the curve
how fine it is
next bit must fit
it will not go
because of the glue
it will not go
the curve is wrong
should have put
the other piece first
press it slightly
a tiny crunch
flakes fall off
bits collapse
it is hopeless
the fine tension
of material and intent and heat
is lost

Obliteration of the mind

Now I begin to know, with age
and the approaching night – I mean
the darkness, the unknowing, the obliteration
of the mind, its ideas and visions,
its fears, beside the desire to create
some tiny monument for another time –
I begin to know or to imagine
how those before us opened their eyes
each morning to the rest of their lives
and the urgent matters of the day.

I thought it easy to examine
the long litany of knowledge
of our predecessors: to imagine
how early man might look forth
from his cave or hut; how Roman
or medieval man would gaze upon
disputed lands; how later, as we begin
to recognise people like ourselves, we seem
to know those poets and artists and musicians
who in the morning might see their stave of notes,
or the argument and the rhyme,
or the colours of the shifting world.

These ideas are foolish fantasies,
they come from those old childhood stories,
of monks and princes, of princesses
and poor working girls, who gazed all
from their windows in hope or misery.
Why should we pretend to understand
the thoughts or plans or fears of those
we admire because their works are famous?
Remember instead what can be learnt
from the past, absorb it, and go further.
Better spend our anxious energies
dispelling fear of mortality,
writing some helpful or amusing lines
before the final darkness falls.
After all, we too have been given,
by chance, our own present moment.

Ode to a cocksparrow

For a sick friend

Lie still, lie still and wait
wait for the rain to stop
wait for the drops to fall
from the leaf onto your page
and raise, and raise –
the word into the light of day.

Flap, flap your tired wings
stamp on the stinking mud
wave your twitching tail
and rise, and rise –
and show us where the beauty lies;
show us where the beauty lies.

Pushing outward

everything pushes outward
each cell remakes itself
with variation
adaptation experiment
extended structures
twigging forth
in adjacent realms
time does not flow
as a quantity in itself
it is merely the duration
of what happens and we
the unforeseen consequences
of accidental conjunctions
we cannot imagine
the activity going on now
the constant pushing outward
as long as there is any
energy
left

The beauty of decay

Here is a brown spot upon an apple
growing steadily each day
at its centre a tiny source of change.
Why feel such visceral revulsion
imagining the beneficial slug
crawling through my eye socket
to make dead visions fertile once again?
Here is a spot upon my skin, perhaps
tomorrow from the unknown centre
it will flower.

The invisible procession

'... an invisible procession going by...'
C P Cavafy, *The god abandons Antony*

We used to be avid for many things
the mind's refinement
or enfolding in another body
to fill the emptiness
We traversed our lifetimes looking
for beauty here or there
so many years expended
some pictures to hang on empty walls

We travelled through deep floods
halfway across the county
some people marooned in the deluge
while we piled through at full pelt
The waters parted and rose up
in walls about us
until we came to the place we didn't know
but for old reasons needed to find

All the time below the house
the foaming river ran brown and lumpy
with fresh earth off the fields
and the boiling of more water coming on
Upstairs in a great light room
material and intent and time
rendered into essence
refined against the grain

The women there with their clear eyes
as if waiting in a garden smiling
the reflection on the persons
we are revealed to be

The present moment

Close your eyes and consider
the image you just thought
to be the present moment:
the trees moving in the wind;
the birds feeding on their crumbs;
or yourself in meditation.
But there is no present moment:
there is only
a moving surface
between past and future;
it is only through duration
that the moment can be seen
and remembered.
Time does not exist, except
as a measurement of change
in things which do exist.

The reason for black holes

Normally you know where things are
which clothes are in each drawer
which things are in each pocket
how much money in your wallet
which papers on your table
these little piles of things arranged
graphically in your mind
like icons on your screen
how then do you deal with failure
with something funny going on
when the system crashes
the utter mystery
of losing something you just had
reduced to searching the same pockets
several times hoping something changes
sifting through the rubbish basket
emptying it on newspaper
recognising discards of yesterday
recurring in reverse
reduced to feeling under furniture
staring obsessively along the street
down in the gutter and up alleyways
all this because a ten pound note
I was holding in my hand at ten o'clock
through some strange hole or passage
dropped into another universe
and I although suspecting alien powers
which accumulate the things we lose
and although quite fond of foreign travel
let go and so was left behind.

The third runway

i.m. William C. Bennett, 1890-1981

Beside the road an empty expanse
escapes across to distant trees,
a flat vista of cracked concrete,
the slabs sometimes separating,
the grass growing through, silent
save for a skylark overhead;
while over at the other side
the camouflaged hangars stand.

The old soldier and his son-in-law
are walking; they pass the expanse
of empty decaying concrete
and the dim hangars over there.
– This runway here, the old soldier says,
was for taking off, the other
at the back was meant for landing.
And he stopped, and stood, and stared.

– Where have you lads been? says grandma.
– We came by the old airfield, says Jack.
– Yes, says her husband, and there
at the far end before the hangars
I saw a couple of aircrews
in their blue uniforms, peaked caps,
and chaps in pilots' helmets,
talking, smoking, heard their voices.

– No, Pop, says Jack, there was no one there;
it's long abandoned and derelict.
– Well, says Pop, I saw them all right;
they'd come in on another runway.

To a sister

Can't remember exactly
how old I was or you
might have been;
it doesn't matter,
it is – it was –
it would have been –
the satisfaction
around that age
in that part of Cheshire
of being able to say:
– hey up, where's our kid?
and: – come on, our kid!
usually referring
to a younger brother
but I needed you
for your feminity
your difference
and of course
the terrific company.
I think you would have been
four years younger;
our mother told me once
and said she had been
digging potatoes
for the war effort.

To Hannah on her 40th birthday

12th November 2015

don't be alarmed
at a strange square number
marking an appointed day
till yesterday your age
was much more curly
made of three thirteens
and next year next year
will bring a prime number
and a sense of freedom

had your dear mother's contractions
arrived sooner or later
this day wouldn't be your birthday
and you would have had
to rearrange this stage
of personal evolution

oh Hannah you are neither
young nor old you are
who you turn out to be
caught as it happens
in the middle of a life
with parents apparently older
and children apparently younger
and all of these identities
without our choosing

enjoy this day of course we like
to celebrate with friends
but as the candles flicker out
remember who you are
remember it is now
it is always now

Towards the edge

i.m. Nick Alexander, d. January 2017

towards the edge
in a clearing
a voice begins to sing

lying among the roots
here is a pebble
or a polished memory

let us hold hands
and pass like ghosts
through the obliterations of mercy

here are the people we used to be
go round shaking hands
smile at those we never were

burning in a clouded sky
the sun is masked by doubt
while the darkening earth rears up

close your eyes and listen
listen as new words form
before the coming of the light

Translation

'Wovon man nicht sprechen kann, darüber muss man schweigen.'
[Whereof one cannot speak, thereon must one remain silent.]
Ludwig Wittgenstein, *Tractatus Logico-Philosophicus.*

We mock a sentence that prohibits itself.
It is the task of thought to think new thoughts,
of language to express the scarce imagined.
Whereof we cannot speak, thereon must we speak.

The absurd instruction sets us free.
We have eaten the forbidden fruit,
we will make the invisible visible,
we will climb forth from limitation.

Through words we are joined together,
we laugh at the possibilities
as we sniff and poke each unknown zone
of new and strange ideas.

Instead of silence we must find
the will to render matter into mind.

Unpoem

… it seemed to be a corridor
curving and extending
into a wider lighter space
with people coming forth
and mingling and moving on
between tables covered with strange things
such as triangular shapes
among festoons and lanterns in the air
with the murmur of voices
from all sides sometimes
calling out: there she is!
there is Arabella Fry!
Was there a person
taller than the others
like the eight-foot man
we saw once in Damascus
with a trail of followers –
one of whom shook hands
and grinned and offered me
a bitter fruit from his paper bag.
So I moved along
in a tide of otherness
amid absurdity
and incomprehension…
yet there was comfort,
and familiarity, and no fear.

IV

Legends

Another oyster

Near a southern coast
pyramids of oyster shells stand
high as trees old as centuries
sucked out by ancient tribes.
In imitation or in continuity
year after year I chuck
my oyster shells on to a pile
a few inches high.
                                        She laughed
rue de l'Ancienne-Comédie
in a little bar she laughed
at the young man
– je te montrerai she said
she being his new friend
showed how to squeeze
a drop of lemon juice
the oyster crinkles at its edge
you know it is alive
the living flesh
the true communion
and after swallowing
the soft lambent blob
you drink from the shell
the liquor of our mother
the ocean.
                              Here is
another oyster press
the knife in and along
turn the blade and feel
the oyster muscle yield
inside there is a kind of pearl

small and grey reflecting
the merest point of light
doubtless formed around
a precious memory
or a piece of grit
and perfectly worthless.

Oh,

throw the shell upon the pile
and perform the ritual again.

Chopping garlic

In Paris
through an archway
in the garage
set for a feast
everybody busy
trestles chairs voices
at a small table
with a sharp knife
I have my task
everyone will eat my task
I am chopping garlic
it is serious
we will commemorate
a teacher's work
all those years ago
chopping garlic
it is getting finer
how I love garlic
it swims in me
it is strength
flowering
growing up
love of women
love of language
it is well chopped

I am proud of it
I take it to some one
she says hmm
now chop it again
with more attention
how did she know
here I am again
holding the knife
watching the blade
the smell rises
the garlic flows
I know nothing
I am empty
time has stopped

Ode to Bukowski

[Charles Bukowski, poet, 1920-1994]

You died dammit
Bukowski no doubt with a lot
of great shit
still inside you and what's more
before passive
tight trouser people
accidentally
came across your stuff
unexpectedly
in a fat book and kind of
delightedly
had to buy it despite
no intention
of spending £20 that morning
$30 to you
we could have spent it
on a drink together
instead of on a pile of
words running
steadily down the page
but you died dammit
Bukowski by the way
that woman whose ass assumed
a curious shape
on the escalator
on page 175
she got off the bus today
in my home town
she looked desirable
she looked right through me

as if you and she and I weren't there
I should have wished her well
in a kindly or apologetic way
like you did once
but she seemed blurred
she seemed blurred
meanwhile
this is an update
for you and the others
in wormy hell
you had the guts to say it dammit
Bukowski when the days
are short and the nights
are black and long you had
the guts to see it
somewhere amid decay
the seasons turn
the seasons turn
and you left sticky traces
of good things
on the mattress
and in the coffin

The golden apples

Turn off the road here
down the slope to the lower level
it's soft at the bottom
engage the four by four
we are in the orchards
the pickers passed last week
apples they have missed
are gleaming on the trees
slowly we pass the ends of rows
ground shining with windfalls
the two girls are perching
in the back of the truck
– hold on tight I shout and
– lie down low branches coming
ripe fruit is falling on us
later we will pick the golden apples
before pressing pulverise them
only then do they give up
their juice in gushes
we move slowly on
past the ruined building
past the old reservoir
the village comes into view
the girls knock on the roof we stop
they have put bandanas on
they are hauling the gun round
cranking it up aiming
the truck rocks and shudders
spits and puffs flicker in the trees
the girls knock on the roof again

we reverse out and head away
in the mirror I see a woman
holding a kind of dart
running fast and catching up
I shout to the girls – throw down
one of the golden apples!
throw down one of the golden apples!
the woman pauses to pick it up
and runs again faster than before.

A low coup

will the master use

the untaught hold to defeat

his pupil's challenge?